TABLE OF CONTENTS

Date	Project	Page
	MY TOOL CHECKLIST	16

Safety Tips

General

- Make sure workshop lighting and ventilation are adequate.
- Keep children, onlookers, and pets away from the work area.
- Concentrate on the job; do not rush or take shortcuts. Never work when you are tired, stressed, or have been drinking alcohol or using medications that induce drowsiness.
- Find a comfortable stance; avoid over-reaching.
- Keep your work area clean and tidy; clutter can lead to accidents.

Hand Tools

- Use the appropriate tool for the job; do not try to make a tool do something for which it was not designed.
- When possible, cut away from yourself rather than toward your body.
- Keep tools clean and sharp.

Power Tools

- Wear appropriate safety gear: safety glasses or face shield and hearing protection. If there is no dust collection system, wear a dust mask. For allergenic woods, such as ebony, use a respirator.
- Read your owner's manual carefully before operating any tool.
- Tie back long hair and avoid loose-fitting clothing. Remove rings and other jewelry that can catch in moving parts.

- Unplug a tool before performing setup or installation operations.
- Whenever possible, clamp down the workpiece, leaving both hands free to perform an operation.
- Keep your hands well away from a turning blade or bit.
- Turn off a tool if it produces an unfamiliar vibration or noise; have the tool serviced before resuming operations.
- Do not use a tool if any part of it is worn or damaged.

Finishing

- Do not eat, drink, or smoke when using finishing products.
- Avoid exposure to organic solvents if you are pregnant or breastfeeding.
- Install at least one smoke detector on the ceiling of your shop above potential fire hazards; keep a fully charged ABC fire extinguisher nearby.
- Never store solvents or chemicals in unmarked containers. Chemical solutions should always be stored in dark glass jars to shield them from light, which may change their composition.
- Store finishing products in a locked cabinet.
- To prevent eye injury, wear safety goggles, and don rubber gloves when working with caustic or toxic finishing products.
- Do not flush used solvents down the drain. Do an Internet search to find out who handles chemical disposal in your area, or check with your local fire department.

Typical Power Tool Wattage Ratings

Tool	Watts (Start-up)	Watts (Running)
Air compressor (¾-hp)	4000	2000
Table saw (10")	4000	1500
Saber saw	2500	1200
Circular saw (7¼")	2500	1200
Circular saw (6½")	2200	1000
Belt sander	1500	600
Bench grinder (½-hp)	1500	1200
Orbital sander	900	360
Router	900	700
Electric drill (½")	800	600
Electric drill (⅜")	600	350
Power plane	600	450
Electric drill (¼")	500	250
Random-orbit sander	500	360
HVLP spray system	400	240

Shop Layout Checklist

Location

- Which available areas in and around your home are appropriate for a shop?
- How easy is the access to these areas?
- Is the electric wiring adequate for powering your tools and lighting?
- How well are the areas heated, insulated, and ventilated?
- Will shop noise disturb other areas?
- If the location is a basement, will the shop be sharing space with a furnace room or laundry room?
- If the location is an outbuilding or garage, how much space is taken up by cars, bicycles, lawn mowers, and so on?
- Does the building or garage have any heating, electricity, or plumbing?
- How secure is the building or garage from theft?

Type of Work

- What type of woodworking projects will you be doing?
- What size are the materials you will need to move in and out of the shop?
- How much space will be devoted to storing lumber and work in progress?
- What stationary machines, portable power tools, and hand tools will you need?
- Are there enough electrical circuits to supply your power needs?
- How many lighting fixtures does your work require?

- How many workbenches, assembly tables, and accessories like tool cabinets, scrap bins, and sawhorses will you need?
- Will local seasonal temperatures and humidity affect your work?
- Will you be doing a lot of finishing work?

Work Habits

- What room temperature will you need to work comfortably?
- What type of light do you prefer for working?
- Will you be working during daylight hours, or will you be using the shop at night?
- Which tools do you expect to use most often?
- Will you be working alone in the shop, or will it be used by another worker? Would that person have easy access to the shop?
- Will you need to lock the shop or keep it off-limits to children or pets?
- How many hours per day do you expect to spend in the shop?
- Is the flooring made of a material that is comfortable to stand on for long periods of time?

Dust Collection

Equivalent Length of System Elements	
DUCT OR FITTING	EQUIVALENT LENGTH (FEET)
Smooth-wall pipe	Actual length
Corrugated pipe or hose	1.5 x actual length
Unflanged duct, hose, or hood connections	10
90° sharp elbow	20
90° curved elbow	10
90° hose bend	10
45° curved elbow	5
45° hose bend	5
Side leg of 90° T	20
Side leg of 45° Y	5

Static Pressure Loss per Foot of Duct at 3500 and 4000 FPM			
CFM	DIAMETER	3500 FPM	4000 FPM
300	4"	.05 in/ft	.07 in/ft
350	4"	.05 in/ft	.07 in/ft
400	4"	.05 in/ft	.06 in/ft
500	5"	.04 in/ft	.06 in/ft

Air Exhaust Volume Requirements for Machines

MACHINE	CUBIC FEET PER MINUTE (CFM)
Jointer (4–12")	300
Disc sander (up to 12")	300
Vertical belt sander (up to 6")	350
Band saw (up to 2" blade)	400
Table saw (up to 16")	300
Radial arm saw	350
Planer (up to 20")	400
Shaper (½" spindle)	300
Shaper (1" spindle)	500
Lathe	500
Floor sweep	350
Drill press	300
Jigsaw	300

Cross Section of a Tree

Viewed in cross section, a tree trunk at first appears to be a fairly homogeneous column of wood, marked by a series of concentric bands called growth rings. However, a close view reveals distinct layers wrapped around each other, some living, some not. At the center is the heartwood, the densest—and dead—part of the trunk. Encircling the heartwood is the paler sapwood, which is surrounded by the cambium, the trunk's only actively growing segment. Beyond the cambium lies the phloem, the inner part of the bark that distributes nutrients generated by photosynthesis in the leaves to other parts of the tree. The cambium's growth accounts for the layers of sapwood that are added each year. As the inner sapwood recedes from the cambium, its pores gradually clog with resins and gums, and turn into heartwood.

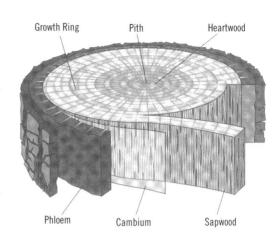

Growth Ring   Pith   Heartwood

Phloem   Cambium   Sapwood

Reading the Grain

Whether you are using a gouge, an adze, or a knife, cutting with the direction of wood grain is critical to the quality of your finished work. The best way to read grain direction is by cutting into it. Working with the grain (top right) yields a smooth, even surface, allowing the tool to easily exit the wood at the end of the cut. Cutting against the wood grain (bottom right) causes the blade to dig into the fibers of the wood, resulting in a rough, choppy surface or causing a deep split in the board. The grain can sometimes be gauged by examining the edge of a board and noting where the grain rises and falls. In general, you should try to cut in the direction of rising grain.

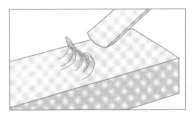

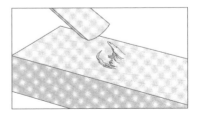

Workability of Wood

Hard

- Apple (*Malus pumila*)
- Ash (*Fraxinus spp.*)
- Beech (*Fagus grandifolia*)
- Birch, white (*Betula papyrifera*)
- Birch, yellow (*Betula alleghaniensis*)
- Cedar, Eastern red (*Juniperus virginiana*)
- Cherry, wild (*Prunus serotina*)
- Dogwood (*Cornus florida*)
- Elm (*Ulmus spp.*)
- Gum, black (*Nyssa sylvatica*)
- Hackberry (*Celtis occidentalis*)
- Hickory (*Carya spp.*)
- Holly (*Ilex opaca*)
- Hornbeam, American (*Carpinus caroliniana*)
- Larch, Western (*Larix occidentalis*)
- Lilac (*Syringa spp.*)
- Locust, black (*Robinia pseudoacacia*)
- Locust, honey (*Gleditsia triacanthos*)
- Maple (*Acer spp.*)
- Mesquite (*Prosopis spp.*)
- Oak (*Quercus spp.*)
- Olive (*Olea europea*)
- Osage orange (*Maclura pomifera*)
- Pear (*Pyrus spp.*)
- Pecan (*Carya illinoensis*)
- Persimmon (*Diospyros virginiana*)
- Pine, Southern yellow (*Pinus spp.*)
- Sycamore (*Platanus occidentalis*)
- Yew, Pacific (*Taxus brevifolia*)

Intermediate

- Alder (*Alnus spp.*)
- Baldcypress (*Taxodium spp.*)
- Chestnut (*Castanea dentate*)
- Douglas-fir (*Psudotsuga menziesii*)
- Gum, red (*Liquidambar styraciflua*)
- Hemlock (*Tsuga spp.*)
- Mulberry (*Morus spp.*)
- Redwood (*Sequoia sempervirens*)
- Sassafras (*Sassafras albidum*)
- Spruce (*Picea spp.*)

Soft

- Aspen (*Populus spp.*)
- Basswood (*Tilia americana*)
- Buckeye (*Aesculus spp.*)
- Butternut (*Juglans cinerea*)
- Catalpa (*Catalpa spp.*)
- Cedar, Northern white (*Thuja occidentalis*)
- Cedar, Southern white (*Chamaecyparis thyoides*)
- Cedar, Western red (*Thujaplicata*)
- Cottonwood (*Populus spp.*)
- Fir, true (*Abies spp.*)
- Magnolia (*Magnolia spp.*)
- Pine, Northern white (*Pinus strobus*)
- Pine, ponderosa (*Pinus ponderosa*)
- Pine, sugar (*Pinus lambertiana*)
- Pine, Western white (*Pinus monticola*)
- Poplar, yellow (*Liriodendron tulipifera*)
- Tupelo, water (*Nyssa aquatica*)
- Willow (*Salix spp.*)

Rockwell Hardness Scales

Scale Symbol	Indenter Type (Ball dimensions indicate diameter.)	Preliminary Force N (kgf)	Total Force N (kgf)	Typical Applications
A	Spheroconical Diamond	98.07 (10)	588.4 (60)	Cemented carbides, thin steel, and shallow case hardened steel.
B	Ball - 1.588 mm (¹⁄₁₆ in.)	98.07 (10)	980.7 (100)	Copper alloys, soft steels, aluminum alloys, malleable iron, etc.
C	Spheroconical Diamond	98.07 (10)	1471 (150)	Steel, hard cast irons, pearlitic malleable iron, titanium, deep case hardened steel, and other materials harder than HRB 100.
D	Spheroconical Diamond	98.07 (10)	980.7 (100)	Thin steel and medium case hardened steel, and pearlitic malleable iron
E	Ball - 3.175 mm (⅛ in.)	98.07 (10)	980.7 (100)	Cast iron, aluminum and magnesium alloys, and bearing metals
F	Ball - 1.588 mm (¹⁄₁₆ in.)	98.07 (10)	588.4 (60)	Annealed copper alloys, and thin soft sheet metals.
G	Ball - 1.588 mm (¹⁄₁₆ in.)	98.07 (10)	1471 (150)	Malleable irons, copper-nickel-zinc and cupro-nickel alloys.
H	Ball - 3.175 mm (⅛ in.)	98.07 (10)	588.4 (60)	Aluminum, zinc, and lead.
K	Ball - 3.175 mm (⅛ in.)	98.07 (10)	1471 (150)	Bearing metals and other very soft or thin materials. Use smallest ball and heaviest load that does not give anvil effect.
L	Ball - 6.350 mm (¼ in.)	98.07 (10)	588.4 (60)	
M	Ball - 6.350 mm (¼ in.)	98.07 (10)	980.7 (100)	
P	Ball - 6.350 mm (¼ in.)	98.07 (10)	1471 (150)	
R	Ball - 12.70 mm (½ in.)	98.07 (10)	588.4 (60)	
S	Ball - 12.70 mm (½ in.)	98.07 (10)	980.7 (100)	
V	Ball - 12.70 mm (½ in.)	98.07 (10)	1471 (150)	
15N	Spheroconical Diamond	29.42 (3)	147.1 (15)	Similar to A, C and D scales, but for thinner gage material or case depth.
30N	Spheroconical Diamond	29.42 (3)	294.2 (30)	
45N	Spheroconical Diamond	29.42 (3)	441.3 (45)	
15T	Ball - 1.588 mm (¹⁄₁₆ in.)	29.42 (3)	147.1 (15)	Similar to B, F and G scales, but for thinner gage material.
30T	Ball - 1.588 mm (¹⁄₁₆ in.)	29.42 (3)	294.2 (30)	
45T	Ball - 1.588 mm (¹⁄₁₆ in.)	29.42 (3)	441.3 (45)	
15W	Ball - 3.175 mm (⅛ in.)	29.42 (3)	147.1 (15)	Very soft material.
30W	Ball - 3.175 mm (⅛ in.)	29.42 (3)	294.2 (30)	
45W	Ball - 3.175 mm (⅛ in.)	29.42 (3)	441.3 (45)	
15X	Ball - 6.350 mm (¼ in.)	29.42 (3)	147.1 (15)	
30X	Ball - 6.350 mm (¼ in.)	29.42 (3)	294.2 (30)	
45X	Ball - 6.350 mm (¼ in.)	29.42 (3)	441.3 (45)	
15Y	Ball - 12.70 mm (½ in.)	29.42 (3)	147.1 (15)	
30Y	Ball - 12.70 mm (½ in.)	29.42 (3)	294.2 (30)	
45Y	Ball - 12.70 mm (½ in.)	29.42 (3)	441.3 (45)	

From *Rockwell Hardness Measurement of Metallic Materials* by Samuel R. Low, published by the National Institute of Standards and Technology, U.S. Department of Commerce

Hardwood Lumber Grades

GRADE	FAS	SELECT	NO. 1 COMMON	NO. 2A & 2B COMMON	NO. 3A COMMON	NO. 3B COMMON
Allowable length of board	8'–16'	6'–16'	4'–16'	4'–16'	4'–16'	4'–16'
Allowable width of board	6" or wider	4" or wider	3" or wider	3" or wider	3" or wider	3" or wider
Minimum % of clear face cuttings	83 ⅓%	83 ⅓%	66 ⅔%	50%	33 ⅓%	25%
Minimum size of clear cuttings	3" x 7'; 4" x 5'	3" x 7'; 4" x 5	3" x 3'; 4" x 2'	3" x 2'	3" x 2"	Not less than 1½" wide containing 36 sq. in.
Formula to determine number of cuts	SM÷4	SM÷4	SM+1÷3	SM÷2	—	—
Maximum number of clear cuttings permitted	4	4	5	7	Unlimited	Unlimited

Reading the Chart

This chart, created by the National Hardwood Lumber Association (NHLA), records the minimum requirements a board must meet to merit a particular grade. Generally, a higher-grade board is longer, wider, and more defect-free than one of a lesser grade. The clear pieces are obtained with as few cuts as possible.

By comparing the dimensions of a board with the figures supplied in the chart, it is possible to determine the grade of a particular piece of lumber. The first two horizontal rows provide data on minimum board dimensions for each grade. The third row gives information on the percentage of defect-free surface, or clear face cuttings, a board must have for each grade. The minimum size of each clear face cutting is listed in row four. Once the surface area, or surface measure (SM), of a board is determined, the formula in row 5 will give the total number of cuttings allowed for a particular grade. Row 6 contains the number of clear cuttings each grade permits.

Shrinkage Values of Different Wood Species

SPECIES	TANGENTIAL (%)	RADIAL (%)	T/R RATIO
Ash, White	7.8	4.9	1.6
Basswood, American	9.3	6.6	1.4
Beech, American	11.9	5.5	2.2
Butternut	6.4	3.4	1.9
Catalpa	4.9	2.5	2.0
Cedar, Alaska yellow	6.0	2.8	2.1
Cedar, Western red	5.0	2.4	2.1
Cherry, black	7.1	3.7	1.9
Douglas-fir	7.8	5.0	1.6
Elm, American	9.5	4.2	2.3
Hackberry	8.9	4.8	1.9
Hickory, shagbark	10.5	7.0	1.5
Holly, American	9.9	4.8	2.1
Madrone	12.4	5.6	2.2
Mahogany, Honduras	5.1	3.7	1.4

(continued on page 12)

SPECIES	TANGENTIAL (%)	RADIAL (%)	T/R RATIO
Maple, sugar	9.9	4.8	2.1
Oak, red	8.6	4.0	2.1
Oak, white	10.5	5.6	1.9
Persimmon	11.2	7.9	1.4
Pine, Eastern white	6.1	2.1	2.9
Pine, ponderosa	6.2	3.9	1.6
Sassafras	6.2	4.0	1.6
Sycamore, American	8.4	5.0	1.7
Teak	4.0	2.2	1.8
Walnut, black	7.8	5.5	1.4
Willow, black	8.7	3.3	2.6

Identifying Grinder Wheels

Standard Marking System Chart			
Abrasive Type	**A:** Aluminum oxide	**C:** Silicon carbide	**Z:** Aluminum zirconium
Abrasive (Grain) Size	**Coarse:** 8. 10, 12, 14, 16, 20, 24	**Medium:** 30, 36, 46, 54, 60	**Fine:** 70, 80, 90, 100, 120, 150, 180	**Very fine:** 220, 240, 280, 320, 400, 500, 600
Grade Scale	**Soft** **Medium** **Hard** A B C D E F G H I J K L M N O P Q R S T U V W X Y Z		
Structure	**Dense** ——————————————➔ **Open** 1 2 3 4 5 6 7 8 9 10 11 12 13 14 15 16 etc.		
Bond Type	**B:** Resinoid **BF:** Resinoid reinforced **E:** Shellac **O:** Oxychloride **R:** Rubber **RF:** Rubber reinforced **S:** Silicate **V:** Vitrified		

Grit Comparison

SANDPAPER	OIL STONES	DIAMOND STONES	WATER-STONES	CERAMIC STONES	MICRON
120	Norton Coarse India				116-97
180	Norton Medium Crystolon		Lee Valley 280		78-68
220		DMT x-coarse, Norton x-coarse diamond	220, Norton 220, Shapton 220		66.82-60
240	Norton Medium India, Norton Fine Crystolon	DMT coarse			53.5-45
280		Norton coarse diamond			43
320	Norton Fine India; Washita		360, Shapton 500		36-29.4
360		DMT fine	Lee Valley 600		29-25
400	Lee Valley Fine India, Norton X-Fine India; Soft Arkansas	Norton fine diamond	600, Lee Valley 800		23-20
600	Lee Valley Soft Arkansas		Lee Valley 1,000, Shapton 1,000		16-14.7
700			Norton 1,000, Lee Valley 1,200	600 or Medium	14-13
800	Hard White Arkansas, Lee Valley Hard Arkansas	Norton x-fine diamond	1,200		12.6-10
1,000		DMT x-fine	1,500		9.2-9
1,500			Norton 2,000, Shapton 2,000	1,800 or fine	8.4-7
2,000	Hard Black or Translucent Arkansas				6

Quick Reference for Formulas

Area of a square ....length x width
Area of a rectangle ....length x width
Area of a triangle .... ½ x base x height
Area of a parallelogram...base x height
Area of a trapezoid .... height x ½(a + b)
Pi (π)... 3.141592, etc., or approx. ²²⁄₇
Circumference of a circle...π x d or 2πr
Diameter of a circle ....C/π
Radius of a circle...C/2π
Area of a circle .... πr²
Area of a sector of a circle... ½ x arc length x r
Motor speed .... 120 x F/P
Work ....F x D
Torque ....F x D
Full-load torque ....hp x 5252/rpm
Horsepower..V x I x Eff/746 or T x rpm/5252
Board feet... (T x W x L)/144

Square

s2

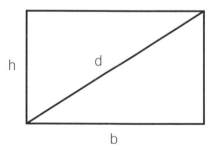

s1

d

s = side, d = diagonal
Example: If s = 14 in.,
then Area = 14 x 14 = 196 sq. in.

Rectangle

h

d

b

h = height or width, d = diagonal, b = base or length
Example: If h = 12 in. and b = 15 in.,
then Area = 12 x 15 = 180 sq. in.

14

Triangle

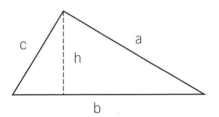

a, b, c = sides; h = height
Example: If b = 17.5 in. and h = 14 in.,
then Area = ½ (17.5 x 14) = ½ (245) = 122.5 sq. in.

Parallelogram

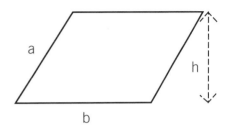

a = side, b = base, h = height
Example: If b = 24 in. and h = 10 in.,
then Area = 24 x 10 = 240 sq. in.

Trapezoid

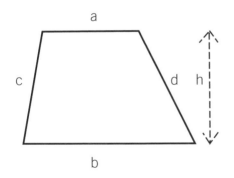

a = one base, b = other base, h = height
Example: If a = 20 in., b = 30 in., and h = 12 in.,
then Area = 12 x ½ (20 + 30) = 12 x 25 = 300 sq. in.

Circle

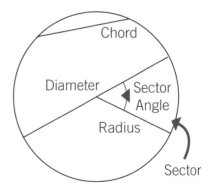

Example: If d = 8, r = 4,
then Area = 3.14 x 4 x 4 = 50.24 sq. in.

Woodworking Tools

BORING

- ( ) **Awl**
- ( ) **Brace**
- ( ) **Center Punch**
- ( )
- ( )
- ( )
- ( )

CLAMPS

- ( ) **Band Clamp**
- ( ) **Bar Clamp**
- ( ) **C-Clamp**
- ( ) **Corner Clamp**
- ( ) **Edge Clamp**
- ( ) **G-Clamp**
- ( ) **Hand Screw**
- ( ) **Pipe Clamp**
- ( ) **Sash Clamp**
- ( ) **Spring Clamp**
- ( ) **Trigger Clamp**
- ( ) **Web Clamp**
- ( )
- ( )
- ( )
- ( )
- ( )

CUTTING

- ○ **Bench Chisel**
- ○ **Dowel Cutter**
- ○ **Drawknife**
- ○ **Froe**
- ○ **Marking Knife**
- ○ **Mortise Chisel**
- ○ **Paring Chisel**
- ○ **Tin Snip**
- ○ **Utility Knife**
- ○ **Wire Cutter**
- ○
- ○
- ○
- ○
- ○

FASTENING

- ○ **Biscuit Joiner**
- ○ **Flathead Screwdriver**
- ○ **Glue Spreader**
- ○ **Phillips Screwdriver**
- ○ **Pincers**
- ○ **Staple Gun**
- ○
- ○
- ○
- ○

17

MEASURING

LOCATION OF TOOL

- Bevel Gauge
- Box Beam Level
- Caliper
- Carpenter's Square
- Compass
- Cutting Gauge
- I-Beam Level
- Laser Level
- Layout Square
- Marking Gauge
- Moisture Meter
- Panel Gauge
- Protractor
- Sliding Bevel
- Tape Measure
- Torpedo Level
- Trammel
- Try Square

POWER TOOLS	LOCATION OF TOOL	BRAND/MODEL	SERIAL #	DATE OF PURCHASE	VALUE
◯ Band Saw					
◯ Belt Sander					
◯ Bench Grinder					
◯ Circular Saw					
◯ Compound Miter Saw					
◯ Drill Press					
◯ Drum Sander					
◯ Jointer					
◯ Jointer Plane					
◯ Mortiser					
◯ Orbital Sander					
◯ Palm Sander					
◯ Pillar Drill					
◯ Planer					
◯ Portable Planer					
◯ Portable Sander					
◯ Power Drill					
◯ Router					
◯ Sabre Saw					
◯ Sanding Machine					
◯ Scroll Saw					
◯ Shop Vac					
◯ Spindle Moulder					
◯ Spindle Sander					
◯ Table Saw					
◯ Thicknesser					
◯					

POWER TOOLS	LOCATION OF TOOL	BRAND/MODEL	SERIAL #	DATE OF PURCHASE	VALUE
◯					
◯					
◯					
◯					
◯					
◯					
◯					
◯					
◯					
◯					
◯					
◯					

SAFETY

	LOCATION OF TOOL
◯ **Disposable Mask**	
◯ **Dust Extraction System**	
◯ **Ear Plugs**	
◯ **Push Stick**	
◯ **Respirator**	
◯ **Safety Glasses**	
◯	
◯	
◯	
◯	
◯	
◯	
◯	
◯	

20

SAWS

- Back Saw
- Bow Saw
- Carcass Saw
- Coping Saw
- Crosscut Saw
- Dovetail Saw
- Dozuki Saw
- Fretsaw
- Gent's Saw
- Gyokucho Ryoba
- Jigsaw
- Keyhole Saw
- Miter Box Saw
- Panel Saw
- Radial Arm Saw
- Rip Saw
- Tenon Saw

- ◯ **Adjustable Mouth Block Plane**
- ◯ **Bastard File**
- ◯ **Bench Plane**
- ◯ **Block Plane**
- ◯ **Bull Nose Plane**
- ◯ **Butt Mortise Plane**
- ◯ **Cabinet Scraper**
- ◯ **Chariot Plane**
- ◯ **Chisel Plane**
- ◯ **Compass Plane**
- ◯ **Iron Rebate Plane**
- ◯ **Iron Shoulder Plane**
- ◯ **Iron Smoothing Plane**
- ◯ **Jack Plane**
- ◯ **Miter Plane**
- ◯ **Moulding Plane**
- ◯ **Plough Plane**
- ◯ **Rabbet Plane**
- ◯ **Rasp**
- ◯ **Rat Tail File**
- ◯ **Roughing Plane**
- ◯ **Router Plane**
- ◯ **Scraping Plane**
- ◯ **Scrub Plane**
- ◯ **Side Fillister Plane**
- ◯ **Smoothing Plane**
- ◯ **Spokeshave**

SMOOTHING

LOCATION OF TOOL

- ( ) **Surface Planer**
- ( ) **Toothing Plane**
- ( ) **Trying Plane**
- ( ) **Warding File**
- ( ) **Wooden Rebate Plane**
- ( )
- ( )
- ( )
- ( )
- ( )
- ( )
- ( )
- ( )
- ( )
- ( )
- ( )
- ( )
- ( )
- ( )

STRIKING

LOCATION OF TOOL

- ( ) **Claw Hammer**
- ( ) **Mallet**
- ( ) **Pin Hammer**
- ( ) **Tack Hammer**
- ( )
- ( )
- ( )
- ( )

PROJECT

PROJECT

Date

PROJECT

Date

PROJECT

PROJECT

Date

Date _____

PROJECT

Date

PROJECT

Date _____

PROJECT

Date

PROJECT

68

PROJECT

Date _____

PROJECT

76

PROJECT

PROJECT

PROJECT

Date _____

82

Date

Date _____

PROJECT

88

Date

Date

Date

PROJECT

110

PROJECT

Date

Date _____

Date _____

PROJECT

Date

Date

PROJECT

Date

NOTES

ISBN 978-1-64178-044-5

Fox Chapel Publishing makes every effort to use environmentally friendly paper for printing.

Fotolia credit: natalitovchenko (endpaper background)
Shutterstock credits: ajt (19); Andrey Eremin (20 top); Baiploo (20 bottom); Icswart (17 top); jiangdi (16 top); kongsky (23 bottom); Ngukiaw (17 bottom); ONYXprj (front cover); Ozz Design (box decorations on front endpaper); rawf8 (23 top); Sashkin (16 bottom); Seregam (22); Vadym Zaitsev (21); Vova Shevchuk (18)

Diagrams and math examples on pages 14–15: from *Woodworkers' Essential Facts, Formulas & Short-Cuts*, by Ken Horner

We are always looking for talented authors and artists. To submit an idea, please send a brief inquiry to acquisitions@foxchapelpublishing.com.

Printed in China
First printing